The Plan,

The Process

And

Procedure

By: Author Shon Gardner

ISBN

ISBN:9781798218433

A PUYOUR POETRY PRODUCTION

Table of Contents

Several things might come to mind when you hear the name Shon Gardner. From styling models, hosting casting calls, creative directing photo shoots, producing fashion runways shows, and I'm also the designer behind my clothing brand Cloud Nine Couture. However, having several years in the fashion industry, I began to develop a critical eye and structured brain for producing and coordinating fashion runway shows.

I've gained tons of knowledge from working alongside some of the best designers, having access to various prestigious fashion events, and studying endless behind the scenes YouTube videos of New York

Fashion Week. Not to mention, I was a featured designer during New York Fashion Week fall 2018. I have had the opportunity to produce and coordinate charity fashion events throughout the Texas area. Some of my most popular shows include; Fashion for Peace, Men of the Hour and Fashion Forward Affair.

Introduction

As an event planner you set the tone for all events. It is your ultimate job to make sure everything will go as planned. Everything matters, especially the smallest details that might go mistakenly overlooked. You want to make sure all things flow smooth sail. When a client comes to you, they're looking for the outlet to make their life easier. You are almost like a personal assistant to their occasion. People will pay for convenience at all cost if they feel it is necessary. How many times have you been to an event and began to wonder why is the check in process so hectic; why were the directions or signage not clear or parking was just terrible? All things must be taken into consideration for your guest. When planning an event I know sometimes things can be a little crazy especially considering on where to start. There are several things to take into consideration.

This guide will be your best friend, almost going down the yellow brick road trying to find your way home, but instead you're going to find the solution to the problem you have always been looking for. Everything in life has a process. Without tools, techniques and strategies, you will be like a kid in a candy store lost and indecisive with too many options. If you're trying to pursue a career in event planning or just want to operate a small business on the side, this is for you.

The Plan

Have clear insight

When planning events, it is almost like having a food recipe. No matter the level of display, certain things are key to having a successful end result. It is very important that you know what elements are required when planning for a client or yourself. Once that is discovered, you will have a clear direction on your final outcome.

You want to map out all the possible details; everything from top, bottom and in between. It's better to prepare for the unexpected. Understanding the vision of the event can go a long way. It will define the atmosphere, food, decor and attendees. Each occasion will vary depending on your client or your personal taste.

Page 7

Ex:

Event Type- Baby Shower

Theme- Duck Tales

Depending on client, some elements might include-

Catering

Decor

Save the dates

Games

Photography

Venue

DJ

Consultation Sheet

Name:_____________________ Today's Date: Month/Day/ Year

Phone: (____) ____-______
Email:____________________@___________

Expected Day of Event: Month/Day/ Year

Event Type: (circle one) Birthday, Baby shower, Fashion Show, Sweet 16, other.

Theme___________________________

Guest Attendee Rang: ______ to ______   Max Budget$__________

Event Details:

____
____
____
____
____
____
____
____
____
____
____
____
____
____

Budgeting

Anything that requires spending money requires a budget. No matter what event you are planning, a budget is always necessary. Sometimes your client may not have a clue of what they want, so then you're left with a big question mark of *"How can I help you...let alone how can you help yourself?"* Budgeting will help you save and not end up in the negative.

It is very important to know where every aspect of money is going so that you won't overspend. Under spending is always good especially if you know how to negotiate, bargain shop or if you're a *"DIY "*(do it yourself) type of person. Being sure of a maximum target number is always best. If you're not a person who is great with numbers; getting various quotes would be best to narrow down your solutions.

Ex: Baby Shower Budget

Guest list ___________________________________ 100
attendees

Max budget___________________________________ $600.00

Budget Breakdown

Catering ___________________________________ $200.00

Decor___________________________________ $100.00

Games___________________________________ $25.00

Photography___________________________________ $75.00

Venue___________________________________ $125.00

Dj___________________________________$75.00

Grand Total___________________________________ $600.00

Knowing what works

When you are self-assured with what works for you or your client, negotiating will be decision making made easy. Having a direction of what you like or what your client is willing to settle for is great! It's like a bride trying to decide on real or imitation flowers; her bridesmaids might have imitation flowers on their bouquets, and the bride might carry a bouquet filled with real flowers.

Sometimes compromise is not the easiest, but it is always best when you have multiple options. Creating a client survey or questionnaire are great ways to get options narrowed down. When you have a sense of understanding what your clients love or you know their personality, this will also help take their vision to the next level.

Process

Time Management and Strategy

Time management is very key to making things work within your life and schedule. Not all events require the same amount of attention depending on the date, season or client, but they do require attention to precise details. When creating the perfect check off list, it is always important to prioritize what is most important to accomplish first. For example; if you have products to order online, you want to gauge the amount of time it takes to arrive.

This will ultimately determine when you should order them. Other methods would be creating a calendar full of deadlines and execute them accordingly. Deadlines will always keep you on top of getting things done with urgency. On average it takes two to three months to effectively plan any event depending on the caliber.

Complete time management exercise below......

Put the below items in chronological order of priority from first to last using numbers 1-7.

Consultation Date- February 2

Event Date- May 11

☐   *Catering*

☐   *Guest list*

☐   *Decor*

☐   *Save the Dates*

☐   *Games*

☐   *Photography*

☐   *Venue*

Resources

Most people or places have their own preference on which you should choose to do business with. Venues like to call it a preferred vendor list. A preferred vendor list is a list of some of the best companies or brands who specialize in certain things, such as catering, décor, photography and more. As you continue to grow in planning events, you will develop business relationships.

Having a list of some of your favorite brand options are great ways to build your own reference guide, and this is a better way to offer your clients a variety of services.

If you're doing an event for yourself or a client chooses a venue that allows outside companies to come in and set up, you can always use your own resources. You always want to get quality bang for your buck. Developing your own guide can always be played to your advantage.

Procedure

Execute

Once you have discovered what is required, finalized your budget and have come to a final solution, now you can begin to connect the dots. On top of creating deadlines, it never hurts to go back and finalize every aspect of the details. As your event approaches, you should have a finalized consultation with your client to review all of your planning notes and make follow up calls just to make sure all changes or updates are solidified.

As a planner, you want to be as thorough as possible. Room for error can cause many problems. Again, time management is very important. The most effective way to execute your event is by creating a timeline. The timeline should consist of all moving parts; such as setup times, date, locations and the flow of the event.

Ex: Event Layout

Date: May 11

Time- 5:30-9:00 pm.

Location- Edison's

Pre-event Setup

Decor set up: 3:00 pm.

Catering arrival: 4:45 pm.

Everything complete: 5:00 pm.

Event Timeline

Mixer: 5:30-6:00 pm.

Arrival Time of the Mother-to-be: 6:00 pm.

Games: 6-6:30 pm.

Food Served: 6:30-7:10 pm.

Presentation of Gifts: 7:10-8:00 pm.

Pictures: 8:00-8:30 pm.

End of Shower/Clean Up: 8:30-9:00 pm

If this was resourceful, stay tuned for my upcoming book *"Structural Elements of Art."* This will connect all of the pieces of the puzzle to the next level. This book will give you knowledge on how to gain sponsorship's, find volunteers, vendors and develop a lifetime of resourceful connections.

For seminar booking inquiries email
StylistShonGardner@gmail.com

Stay connected by following

 Draeshyn

 Stylist Shon Gardner

 Shon Draeshyn Gardner

Notes